Go West, Young Woman

by Georgie Abel

For Gus and Scout

Author's Note

Hey. Hey you, yes you with the tingling palms, the forehead wrinkles, you, you love coffee, you, the mess up, the never says the right thing, the fearful, the when are you ever gonna get your shit together, the hangry and the road rager, you, yes you, the one who falls in love with people at Trader Joe's, you, you sweet awkward thing, the here comes trouble, the oh my god if you only knew, you're so able to be loved, it's easy, you, you want tacos right now, and you, you always try to make people feel included, that is so important, the skinny jeans don't fit anymore you, the hungover you, the not over it yet you, how raw and how true, you're the most honest thing I've ever seen, and you, the shadow you, the one swimming in darkness, gulp it down faster now, you, the you that can't say sorry, the stubborn you, the never gonna let go of that one you, you earth dream, you try so hard, so much, so deeply, in so many different ways, you try, barefoot in your driveway, you try like the world was gonna end, like you were just born, you've tried for so long, spent your life trying you, failing you, the best you can do you, always fighting for it, resilient as ever you, you, tired you, exhausted you, down for the count, you, you warrior, you always higher, up, towards the heavens, climbing, get me off of the earth you, never resting you, never still you, always testing you, like a storm, like a mosquito, like a mango, like your 4th grade teacher, like dandelions, you, yes you. You are someone's reason for believing in god.

I hope that this book reminds you of who you are.

All my love,
G

girl child

the sand was still cold from nighttime, it was morning

and we were allowed to go to the beach alone.

we put sand down the fronts of our one-pieces

forming two mounds over our young chests

paraded around with our hands on our hips

and our shoulders thrown back.

"someday,"

we said.

the sand slid down our bathing suits

and gathered into a hill at our bellies

that we lightly pressed our palms against.

"someday,"

we said.

the sand did not come out easily.

it sifted between the bathing suit and its mesh liner,

so she said,

"I know!" and took my hand, jerked me towards the sea

we were running

and I knew it was going to be cold but I didn't care and when we reached the water

we just kept running until the ocean took our legs out from under us and we floated

the waves were gentle and we ducked our heads under the surface

where things were a whole lot quieter.

I remember her hair, suspended in that darkness and fanning out, away from her.

we came up for air, she spit and wiped her nose with the back of her hand

she said,

"I wanna stay eleven years old for as long as I can,"

and I thought that even though her Mom probably told her to want that, that was exactly what I wanted too.

earthquake weather

out in these parts, no one slept past seven.

shook out of sleep by a great primordial moan,

our eyes opened in unison.

waking together, a collective question was posed:

is this The Big One?

our backs hardened, our pupils grew wide

and we all looked for a pair of pants

as the earth arched her spine and banged her fists against our walls.

cracks in the crust,   exposing something deeper,

tremors in the framework,   that act as our skeleton,

an upheaval of the foundation,   that we've built everything upon

a reminder   from something subterranean

that we are not in charge here.

wake up, she dares us,

all together now.

trail dance
eastbound and midmorning,
i'm running through the hills, in a sense,
but a better verb for what I do out there is
dance.
my body, three sixty spinning as I do the electric slide,
and my hips, they dip, into the land and
I bob my head, Martha Graham,
and kiss the back of my hand. I blow it west.
The trees are doused in glitter and
I John Travolta all over their branches,
pause for a moment, hold different stances
like the robot,
don't you remember how it used to be?
the ground is muddy
these days
and on the downhills,
I call it moonwalking but really I'm just losing traction,
give me some Michael Jackson,
my feet slide, cut through the earth
as it gives birth
to the most true scent,
wet eucalyptus,
and here comes Prince,
my hand finds my heart
my hips find my spine
as I Shakira Shakira through the moss.
I square dance with the fog.
I am a compass,
I spin with blurred vision
but always know where I am cause
east, west, north, south,
here, right here is where i land
cause baby i'm earth-bound,
mouth like James Brown,
moving among the wild things
that each season brings
and you don't see them feeling sorry for themselves.
remember? there is bass in the woods.
and unlike human song, it's always dropping

synapsing your movement and popping
your arms like you got electrocuted
when was the last time?
you gave in?
you've already got your bearings
just trust the spin.

jack kerouac

he said,
give me jack kerouac.
give
me jack
kerouac.
give me—
give me jack,
give me jack
        motherfucking kerouac.
she heard it in a laundromat.
slammed her fist
on the dryer and
threw her head back
as she yelled
        god
                        damnit!
someone get this man
some jack kerouac!
she came to her senses.
tears still salty on her cheeks.
she remembered, she knew, from way way back,
what she had—
she had some
jack kerouac.
as a matter of fact—
she was made
of jack,
made of jack
kerouac.
finally, she exhaled, a man
who wanted her poetry.
but she had placed it somewhere deep,
somewhere black,
where, she wondered, was
her jack kerouac?
it had to be around here somewhere.

so she emptied her pockets,
lint and a tick tack,
but laughed at herself because it wasn't
somewhere like that,
it was in her voice
her sound,
her soundtrack,
yes, she remembered,
she knew right where it was at,
so she cut open her chest and
pouring out of her
came
jack, puddles on the floor
of jack
kerouac.

equinox
i see you.
you are half
and half
exactly
not even saying that
abstractly
you,
you equinox babe,
you are moon and you are sun
you are bullet and you are gun
you are old and you are young
and you,
i see you.
always have.
always do.
you've been walking around town
like the winter wasn't shit
spitting rhymes
like cherry pits
oh damn, oh lord, oh my
i see you.
you equinox babe,
you are yin and you are yang
you are night and you are day
you are growth and you are decay
hundreds
of thousands
of pressed wildflowers are what
make up your vertebrae.
you equinox babe,
got rainwater flowin' through your lymph nodes
tree sap for blood
just one word of yours causes a flood
because you say things like
hi sweet one.
you equinox babe.
you are black and you are white
you are left and you are right

you are dark and you are bright
dang.
do it some more, please,
i want your folklore
how'd you get these rains to pour
you equinox babe?
tell me about balance
level
equal
about how if your head won't move
then those feet will
how if you don't know it
that you'll bleed until
ain't nothing left
but bone.
and go on look
at what a mess you made
you earth dream,
you equinox babe.

springtime crazy (originally published in the Climbing Zine)

we've got that springtime crazy,

our hearts have grown hungry under desert skies.

we wanna

take shots of lightning and use thunder to make heavy hip

hop beats

frost a cake with the snowcapped peaks

scoop the cookies and cream stars from the sky and press

them on   a waffle cone

just one taste of these vanilla bones and

we're

addicted to the blooming   cactus, we

know it won't last us

because the summertime   is coming

but for now we

sip the springtime rains, ring out the clouds with open

mouths

and chug their milky nectar

because we've got that springtime crazy,

our hearts have grown hungry under desert skies.

we wanna

throw a slab of sandstone on the grill

sizzling and popping just like the   blood

of our hungry hearts, the thrill

to just be breathing!

synapsing and loud,

and now,   we crave a sage salad

dressed with the sap from a pine,

and a side

of yucca fries

sprinkled with our salty tears,

mined from these wild eyes

because we've got that springtime crazy,

our hearts have grown hungry under desert skies.

give us the moon!   the waxing moon,

we know the moon,

how her face can be caramelized and sliced,

sprinkled with a wildflower spice

and her craters are filled with a cream,

heavy and sweet

been surviving off those moon beams,   oh God

we can't get enough

the dark of winter left us   so ravenous

because we've got that springtime crazy,

our hearts have grown hungry under desert skies.

we wanna

talk about this new space   within us

fill it up with by letting   indian paintbrush

melt on our tongue

ah, to be this young!

we take the needles from a   cactus, push them into

our spine,

bathe our nervous systems in

a brackish brine

cause we want something with desert resilience

to make up our backbones   and you know it's

because we've got that springtime crazy,

and these hearts of ours,

these throbbing hearts of ours,

have grown so hungry,

and of infinite size,

under these ever-changing desert skies.

thunderstorm in telluride

i could smell it coming.

it was summertime and I was alone.

those mountains hold sweetness and scent

much differently than the sierra.

they hold the smell of wildflower and mud like a mother

would hold a child,

an embrace.

the Sierra doesn't do that.

her arms are open and wide, fingers

splayed like the sun rays you drew with crayon

in the corner of the paper you were given

by your babysitter

saying, go,

you must go,

there is too much to see for you to stay here in my arms,

too much love and too much pain,

and once you find all the ways in which your heart

can break

nothing will

ever feel so yours.

thunderstorm at clark mountain

we could smell it coming.

it inked the clouds, dark and heavy

against

a metallic sky.

it turned the landscape silver,

stilled the air and suspended our breath

as we waited

for the inevitable.

the whole thing made me itch.

the sky churned

and twisted

and telescoped

just like his belly,

because

he could smell it coming,

and the tightness of his throat told him

that it was inevitable.

thunderstorm in tuolumne

she could smell it coming.

she said, we should get out of here

but i wanted to stay.

just a little further,

so we walked into the meadow between the Echoes

and

Cathedral Peak.

she said, okay let's turn back now

but i needed something from the high country

and I didn't care

if the clouds shattered

on my shoulders.

thunderstorm at lime kiln canyon

we could smell it coming.

and my thighs were stained with heavy drops already.

i tied into the rope anyway,

the air was electric, I had to.

the subtle bumps in the limestone were wet

and slick but

thunder cracked above my head,

and as I looked up a drop of rain fell into my eye

like Visine

and my vision got clear, I could see colors

that weren't there before, indigo,

it was all indigo,

and I moved without thinking,

moved with the same force that beats my heart and

grows my hair, I swear

something else

was lifting me up the soaked face

I was a puppet

and finally free.

thunderstorm in savannah

the kittens could smell it coming.

i think.

huddled under my bed, four glowing eyes

so still as round after round

of thunder and bright lightning shook the frame

of our old house.

they were so young,

and i wanted so badly to tell

them that they were going to be okay

but there was no way,

i was too human

so on the floor is where i stayed,

belly down

i fell asleep

as the gutters filled with water

and wind threw rain against the window—

i was dreaming, and

woke with two kittens pressed

and breathing

contoured to the curve

of my side.

thunderstorm in appalachia

i could smell it coming.

i had been in a bad mood for a few years and

the sky was sick of it.

give it up girl,

she said.

quit yer fussin' already,

she said.

your fear bores me to tears,

she said.

she rained on my forehead and

i knew it was time.

my mask ran down my cheeks, dripped off my chin

and splattered into my open palms

and for the first time

maybe ever

i let it run through my fingers

and as it seeped into the red mud

she said,

oh thank God.

thunderstorm in wyoming

we could smell it coming.

god, could we smell it coming.

the sky had been holding on for days, threatening

to pour out its insides but it was patient.

it was when the clouds were bursting at their seams that

i met him for the first time.

i didn't know him, and then i did.

after just one word

a strand of lightening spindled between my chest

and his

so strong that it scared me

so magnetic that i had no choice

and i enjoyed the pull.

the rain flooded the grassy hillside into a vast ocean,

and we both ducked under the surface,

we were swimming,

breathing underwater as we marveled in

the way the other moved.

solstice

i take heart
i take heart,
i take heart,
in how i was
face up with moonlight
on my face
and he was
face down with moonlight
on his back
and there was
moonlight woven between us
moonlight being made
moonlight, it stayed
with me
even today
on the longest day
i can use it as breath
use it as evidence
that summer exists,
and will always return,
always yearn,
because of how my hair turns
unruly with heat. unearth me. unfurl me.
because i've got honeybees flowing
straight from my ovaries
because of this solstice
the solstice in my throat
solstice in my my lungs
solstice dissolving on my tongue
solstice when i was just a young
girl.
when i was a young girl
i had me a cowboy
but now,
boy i felt that
solstice on your palm
and i've got that solstice that longs
for your poetry.

we aren't meant to be alone.
i want to cycle with you,
cycle with each other,
so give me another
night like that
give me another
midday taking cover
in the shade
face down now, the both of us,
face down with shade on our backs
face down
bellies pressed against the desert floor
like snakes
but warm blooded, wanting more
like snakes
but with venom that we learned pour
and release without harming
the other
folklore
like snakes
giving thanks to this season
like snakes
face down, ears pinned against earth
listening for
solstice, and now it's here,
faces facing each other
one inch away
eyes closed
drifting into dream
his breath braiding into mine
feeling the heat of his blood
and of his story
a vortex i could agree to
i dreamed
of solstice, of he, of me,
of heat,
calves tanned by gold
and for the first time i stood
on a summit and didn't wanna
scream

into the vastness.
i take heart
in all the ways
we face
each other.
i take heart in this season,
in this ripeness.
in this love of mine.
i take heart,
i take heart,
i take heart.

wyo love

people ask me:

georgie,

who are you writing about

in your poetry?

honey, the answer is easy:

it's about you all,

it's about you doll,

it's you, it's always you,

because you,

you are the salt of my earth.

you are love of my life.

you make the strife around here

a reason to believe in god.

you make the hate

a reason to hug each other for five minutes straight,

(do that if you haven't today)

and i swear to you, the doves are coming.

do you know about that wyo love?

it's all over these parts,

got it all over my heart

like i'm on drugs, like moth love,

like a lady bug

but more earthbound,

tangled in the planet is where is where i found

you,

you earth dream, you high country stream,

salt of my earth,

love of my life,

you got that wyo love

in the palm of your hand

from the fat of land,

you pressed it against my tongue

and it dissolved like a shooting star,

sizzled like a shooting star,

star death, on the crest

of the canyon, it salted the sky that night,

love

of

my

life,

that night

we fell asleep laying on the old highway

that night that lifted into day

that night, i still crave

your eyes, your eyes

are made of rosewater

and a brackish river,

salt

of

my

earth,

and as the nights grow hotter

i slip into july like an oversized t-shirt

writing love letters all day

saying hey hey hey

to everyone i see.

you life loves. you earth salts.

you and me babe,

let me turn us into poetry,

let me tell you about

all the ways in which we haven't failed each other.

let me tell you about

all the ways in which the world isn't yet over.

I know I know, there's evidence that it is, that we're done,

every day, every goddamn day these days, i'm stunned

by this starving planet.

but hold on tight,

loves of my life,

salts of my earth,

joy is coming, joy is here,

cause you're here

to teach me love, and i'm here

to teach you love,

that wyo love,

that quiet love, safe love,

that slow love that you know so well,

like when you were just a child,

salt of my earth!

love of my life!

reminds you of how wild

you actually are, so give it up girl.

let your tightly folded corners unfurl

and get some air, let your hair

grow past your shoulders,

let that wyo love salt your earth,

then

give that shit away

every day, give more,

till you can feel their heart synapsing with yours,

smoldering with purpose, true with the fact

that we belong here,

that we belong together,

that we will save each other

with this love,

with this gentle tug of summer birth.

you love, you are the love of my life,

and

you are the salt of my earth.

waxing

we ate cherries under a waxing moon

spit their pits into the golden grass

and i wondered: had i ever envied stone fruit before?

because in this moment, i did.

how i wanted him to take my heart

into his mouth and remove the deep red flesh

from the seed with

his teeth and tongue

and spit my clean soul into the tall grass so it

could shimmer in the moonlight,

bathe in her white hue,

and i wanted to do the same to him.

i wanted us to chew off all the veils, the masks, the pride, the armor

and just be next to each other in the grass.

he reached over and held my wrist so gently

played with my bracelet as he looked up to the moon.

waxing?

he asked,

and I nodded.

we faced each other, his eyes caught the cool moonlight

and he said,

hi,

as if he was seeing me for the very first time.

walmart parking lot (originally published in the Climbing Zine)

I was this close

to forgetting what it feels like

to sleep in a Walmart parking lot.

Somewhere in between totally fine and

rock bottom,

but probably rock bottom because

you're totally fine

listening to Radiohead and eating barbecue chips

with the covers kicked off,

because it's Wyoming, because it's August.

Look at you, your hair's getting long,

you're moving without thinking about it for three days straight

(that's a charming new development!)

the summer's buzz

was loud enough to drop you down

into your body

like you've wanted for so long,   and now

that you're there,

and you've quit telling yourself that you should really meditate and stretch and

save the whole world

you can be totally fine

sleeping in a Walmart parking lot,

and come to think of it,   that's all

you've been searching for all these years,

to sing with the chorus,

FOR A MINUTE THERE, I LOST MYSELF, I LOST MYSELF

loud enough that someone might even tell you to keep it down,

because it's past midnight,

and there are other people trying to sleep

in a Walmart parking lot.

The Mystery I Never Solved

I always could taste the melancholy on your skin and smell the sadness on your breath. I didn't mind. I did not see you as my joy factory. I was in it for this and this alone: to see you. I thought that this was the whole point.

Within hours, I peeled back the skin of my chest, opened up my ribs like sliding glass doors and said, look, here it is.

But sometimes you would look off in the distance. Sometimes you asked if I could put it away.

I understood. Too fast. Too much. Too broken. Too dark.

I kept trying. Sometimes daily. But even things close to my surface scared you.

So I learned to be patient.

In this manner, years went by.

I birthed five million words of how worthy you are. Poems, letters, lists, and birthday cards that told stories of your goodness. I told you over countless glasses of wine that you are made of magic. While cooking dinner I would remind you of your divinity. I made lists of the people who are in love with you and ran out of paper. My pen went dry. My voice grew hoarse. But I still shouted all of it from my car with the windows down. I held you, I saw you, and I put you back where you belonged–among the redwoods, among the wild mountains. But you never could sleep. We walked through the neighborhood at 3am. You did not want to hold hands but you wanted me to be beside you. We ended up in the park, you were face down in the grass. Like always. With your eyes fixated on the dark earth, you did not know that the moon was at your back. She was illuminating the skin of your elbows and glowing your hair. I told you all of this. This is what I sang to you. It became all that I did.

All the while I was so curious about your closed doors. I thought if I showed you mine, you would show me yours. I wanted to so badly to see the places where you did not want to be touched. I wouldn't touch them, I just wanted to know them. I wanted all of you. I begged for your darkness and craved your bermuda triangles.

But you did not know how to not be alone.

The way that I wanted you angered the place in your spine that told you stories of unworthiness. Because of this, you never really liked me. I was too honest. I was a mirror. I was that tiny voice in your belly that you hadn't heard since you were a child. I was the part of you that still loved yourself.

I wish I could say that I was never afraid to fly away, but I was. I was an addict for this. I wanted to save you because I saw gold in your eyes, and because I wanted to be the hero. I needed someone to be and you gave me a hat to wear that felt important.

Eventually we just got too tired. Our hands withered. Our ankles got creaky. Our throats like a hangover. I pulled my heavy body into my bed and slept for not nearly long enough. But I can laugh. I can speak your name. I am feeding myself. And I trust my life.

You are the mystery I never solved. You are the question I never answered.

2015

years are like lovers—
i can still remember the smell of 2011 and
the way 2009 stole the covers,
i know how 2013 stripped off her sundress and ran
into the mediterranean
and how in her eyes was something subterranean
and 1999, how he held my earlobe when we watched TV,
and of course i miss them but it's not with a heart
that's heavy
it's with a tip of my hat, a nod of my head
both hands on my ribs as I lay in bed.
I can still hear your voices.
but 2015,
2015,
2015 was drinking gasoline
and taking shots of lightning
2015,
you got me unstuck and
2015 was the year i stopped giving a fuck
i flew through the air held by voices of lovers past
i woke up from a spell that had been cast
upon me, seriously,
and i'm down on earth again but i walk so ferociously
i grew roots that are thick and pump water up into my trunk
luck
or fate,
don't know, don't care
give me the ones who can smell history in the air
and who can tell me stories
of this sadness.
give me so many nights tangled
in
your
legs.
these days I don't want to make anything other than love,
because making promises is problematic,

and making commitments is contradictory
and those kind of things are born only to soothe fear
and to give us something invisible to steer
2015,
2015,
you can promise to be honest
and commit to your spirit
but that's all,
and that's it.
so listen hard baby,
this is something that I mean:
let me tell you all of the ways in which we did not fail each other.
let me tell you all of the ways in which we did not fail ourselves.
i'm no better now at saying goodbye than i was before,
but that's the way i want it,
i don't ever want to get good at losing
i want your bermuda triangles and your bathroom floor
so 2015,
2015,
give me something that looks similar to your sheen
but I don't want to keep you
couldn't if i wanted to,
you're gone now, it's over,
and i've got me,
but cheers to you for planting so many seeds,
you crazy,
electric,
bitch!
2015, 2015,
you were bad in all the good ways,
goodbye to you,
I love you now and always,
my darling, catastrophic 2015.

the swagger flu
felt tired for a year and a half, didn't really give

many damns

or birthday gifts

didn't wear many dresses

or hearts on my sleeve

hardly looked in the mirror

didn't really have much to say

couldn't just sit and breathe

barely wrote any poems

no live music

danced maybe twice

bailed a lot.

then, one night i got sick

of it.

chills ripped through my back, and I knew.

I got in bed

and just decided:

okay you nasty ass flu,

come at me bro,

you're gonna make me feel like doodoo but I'm gonna use you

to get my swagger back.

Let's do this shit.

barely walking, five days:

the rest reminded me to always rest

the chills rattled the doubt from my bones

the cough got all the stagnation out of

my heart,

i made room.

and the fever, the fever lit it all on fire.

my brain got hot

and started thinking these new thoughts

like how come you don't go to cafes by yourself anymore

when did you stop reading and

where is your yoga mat.

the fever sparked this coil at the base of my spine

invited it to unwind and made it flow like an electric river

blue and hot

here we go, i thought.

I needed something so I tried this new thing for me

called asking:

help, i said. and they did:

she said—you're Georgie Fucking Abel,

and all that bullshit, that ain't for you, G,

she said—be sweet to yourself,

she said—your gut, I'd go with that,

she said—take care of yourself,

she said—you can't just wither and die,

she said—it's just time.

so I said—you see this here, this here is The Line.

he said—you look

different, more sure of yourself

more calm.

I said—thanks, I finally feel like myself again, that flu really took it out of me,

and we both knew

what I meant by that.

love never fails

love never fails,
love never fails,
got my voice back
and i'm telling you
that love
never fails.
got a loverbabe givin me air
got that love riding on my coattails
got that love gettin' the stale air
out of my lungs
out of my nails
lifting the veil and
love singing me into oblivion
yeah just like corinthians:
"don't give up on love,
cause that shit never fails" (-god)
goddamn
god i am
god am i
seeing god in the palm of your hand
got plans
to slide my fingertips down
your spine, reading your vertebrae
like braille
like oh hell damn,
here we go again
can i phone a friend
can i get a witness
can i get a prayer
but this time i know that
love never fails
love never fails
sure go ahead now
look at all these layers,
i dare you to look at this one,
are you seeing this love
this new blood
this new love

who spends his night
soothing my hip-hop tastebuds
and i've been
riding round town like
the winter can't touch me
this one feels holy
the whole me wants the whole he
whole love
honest love
tell the truth, tell the truth, tell the truth,
to always tell the truth
so help me
cause truth is my favorite style
get off on truth
and yeah i fought it for a little while
but here i am
here we are
already missing
his eyes
so listen
love never fails
love never fails
been broken a thousand times
but i'm telling you
this time
every time
love never fails
love never fails,
trust in this one
in every one
cause when it comes
to love,
that shit
never
fails.

Men I've Carried Out of Deserts (originally published in the Climbing Zine)

I carried him out of the Mojave. Primordial screams bounced off the desert domes, sounds of a broken bone, a future dissolved. His cries are stuck out there, braided into the maze of granite and tangled in the yucca. Go to Barker Dam at dusk. You'll hear it.

Joshua Tree is a skeleton. Not even a map. The spirit of the land roams free, it isn't trapped by physics or humanness. It makes me jealous. How I crave the freedom of not having a body, of being a ghost. Just a framework. Not even a map. Joshua Tree is a skeleton.

They look at me and do not see a woman. I am a joy factory. A wife. A mother. A way for their lives to feel normal. Something to worship and pray to. They know I want to be the hero. So we strike a deal, an offer too good to pass up: save me, and I'll save you.

I start to wither, and they feel strong. This works for a while. I tell myself that this is what good women do. That thirst is selfish. But then I feel a small pulse in my belly. It illuminates everything in faint flickers, but there is enough light for me to know. What should be rooted is weightless and arid.

I reach for water, gulp it down. With one sip I can feel the blood in my legs. Half a glass and I remember that I have feet. This worries them. They begin by threatening small things, and then everything. They start tracking me. They always want to know where I'm going.

I am uninteresting to them once I know how to move on my own. They try to bring me back, pressing spines of cactus into my arm. *You don't know how to move through the desert,* they'd whisper. But it always sounded more like *please babe, I love you.*

How am I supposed to act when these granite walls don't care if you fall? Your flesh dissolves as they siphon the blood from your wrists. They wonder what these walls would say if they could talk but I wonder what I would say if I could talk to these walls. The rocks hold a secret, an answer that I need. They don't save or hold anything. No heroes. Just a framework. Not even a map. Joshua Tree is a skeleton.

It would end quietly. I no longer knew how to scream. I crawled into bed and rested for not nearly long enough. But I can move in the desert. I can laugh with the coyotes at dusk. I can let my dark underbelly slide across the cold desert floor. I know how to breathe off of darkness.

how the desert got her layers

we sit on our front porches and
drink coffee.
we want to paint.
we want to paint the layers of the desert
because her blood is heavy
and opaque,
and we know all about that.
this is a pain we know.
we could do it from memory.
because this is the marrow of our bones.
we know how her layers rose
because
the desert chose
what should go
and what should stay.
she knows how to lose everything.
we know this too.
we know how to do the most unspeakable
act: to kill what needs to die.
we do this every month.
we do this every breath.

this makes us so dangerous
that they've tried to contain us, shame us
into believing that we're mad.
but this is the one thing they can't
take because
these aches,
these aches are the truest thing we know.
our wombs throb
from yet another
violation
of body
of trust
of truth.
space that is taken
again, again, and again.
this never stops for us.

this is life for us.

but this isn't heard. because
they don't know.
they don't want to know. and
a dismantling of privilege
can feel like oppression.
so let this be a lesson in
all the blessings brought to you by
nothing
more
than chance and connections.
your life has so little to do with your own volition.
is this the worst news?
not for a womb,
not for an organ
that knows how to lose.
and our layers are built on
the things we've lost.
slowly they grow into
something our spines can
lengthen from.
even though our stories
have been burned or written
as villain
we still know about all the women
who knew.
their stories, ancient and old,
they are too true for us not to hear.
they are unable to be forgotten.
so we smirk at your endless lies.
we know about every lie you have ever told.
we know this because deep in our bellies,
in our bones,
we have a truth
that for you
is
so rare.
we can see it in our grandmother's hair,
and in our daughter's first pair

of blue jeans.
we have always known.
because
our bodies tear
from this.
we fall to our knees in prayer
from this.
our lungs fill with air
from this.
the desert got her layers from this.

Go West, Young Woman

Go west, young woman, and grow up with the country.

What we need now is for you to manifest your own destiny. Go west young woman, if only in heart. You are the salt of this earth. You are the love of this life. This land uses your lungs to breathe. Young woman, you must go west. Grow the country.

Go west, young woman. Turn towards the sunset and start walking. You know what to bring. You know what you need. Anything you've forgotten, you'll find. Just pack your bag. You'll lose everything anyway, someday.

This losing won't be scary once you get yourself out west. Because your journey will remind you that you're good at losing. You've done it since you were a little girl.

Go alone, go quietly. Go west, young woman. Grow the country.

As you go west, you will be tugged and pulled in all directions. You will be tricked into cutting off your hands. You will blindfold yourself, arms outstretched to those more injured than you. They'll smell you from a mile away. You will think it's love, it will feel like love, but deep down you will always know. They are bad for you. You'll guzzle gasoline, anything, to mask that knowing. But young woman, you're on your way out west. Nothing can stop you for too long. It's just a matter of time.

Save yourself now to save yourself some time.

You will learn that "unconditional love" is a phrase made up by someone who wanted to act badly without consequence. It applies only to your babies and yourself. That's just biology, survival of the fittest. So go west young woman, go west. Make your love conditional as hell.

Go west, but rest for a while after you've been captured. You're injured now, but not for long. You are hardwired for healing. Resilience is your middle name. Now you know that there is no prince coming to save you. You are your own medicine. You always have been. It's all coming for you.

Young woman, sometimes you will go downwards, on your way out west. In your own darkest seasons, you will be pulled underground. Don't fight this. You've always known how to breathe underwater. You know how to dream in the dark. You don't need light to see. Don't prevent the stillness. Rest often. Exhale. Go west.

Just a few miles left to go until you're out west, they will try to pull you back into your state of needing. Because they don't like women like you. They will call you dangerous. They will try to convince you that you've gone mad. There will be please-babe-I-love-yous. They will sink their teeth back into your arm and release their metallic poison. You'll fall for it again and again. Be gentle here. Forgive yourself always, but don't stop. You're so close. Take yourself all the way west, go west, and the lies will hurt your teeth. Go west, tune your ears for truth. Go west young woman. Grow the country.

Out west, that ruby you have in your belly is polished and beaming. There are diamonds dripping down your spine. You are a woman of spirit. You look like a really fun wedding date. You go to cafes alone. You see poetry in the mountains. They look at you like you're the most human thing they've ever seen.

Young woman, I know you're tired, but we need you to go west. Go west, grow our country.

Go west young woman, grow the country between your ribs, in the palm of your hand. You're not a maiden anymore. You don't need their attention, you have you. This will burn anything toxic, watch it all fall away. Good people will come to you. Joy will rise in your eyes from small wonders, the indigo morning. Your sadness will be seeped in spirit. You're a mother now, older than the redwoods. Welcome home.

Thank you for reading. To check out more of Georgie's writing, go to:
https://georgieabel.wordpress.com
https://medium.com/@georgieabel

Made in the USA
Columbia, SC
21 March 2018